"WHO DO *YOU*

A Study Of The Messianic Secret

All Scripture passages are taken from: "The Didache Bible, with commentaries based on the Catechism of the Catholic Church." Ignatius Bible Edition, 2020, and also from: "The New Catholic Study Bible, (NCSB), St. Jerome Edition." Thomas Nelson Publishers, 1985.

ISBN 979-8-218-33983-8

Printed in the United States of America

CONTENTS

Introduction

As described in Scripture, evil entered this world through the fallen angel, Satan, because he succeeded in persuading the first human beings, Adam and Eve, to disobey God thereby committing what the Catholic Church calls Original Sin: the first sin committed by the first human beings. This resulted, of course, in the breakup of the intimate relationship they had enjoyed with God, the Loving Creator of all things. The repair and restoration of this broken relationship between God and mankind was finally achieved 2000 years ago by the suffering, death, and Resurrection of Jesus the Christ, who was – and is forever – both God and man in one Divine Person; the Son of God the Father.

This astounding phenomenon and miracle, that God made for Himself a human body, entered it, and lived with it and in it until adulthood, and then allowed Himself to be brutally tortured and executed like a common criminal in front of hundreds of witnesses is not only a historical fact with plenty of hard evidence to prove it, but also the perfect way He Himself chose to save the human race from Eternal doom in Hell because of Sin. This is extremely mysterious!

The coming of Jesus into the world with this horrible salvific mission as the primary objective and Main Mission was prophesied by Old Testament Prophets throughout the centuries, so it really should not have come as a surprise that Jesus was the foretold Messiah to those who were familiar with the Holy Scriptures; namely, the Pharisees, the Sadducees, and the scribes. But that is precisely what happened! They not only rejected Him, but they treated Him like a common criminal and then had Him executed as well. This mysterious and stark reality, together with other

1

curious data I found in Scripture, finally led me one day to the conclusive question:

Why didn't these "experts" realize–and therefore believe–that Jesus was the promised Messiah? After hundreds of years of prophecies about Him, including where He was going to be born and by whom; what His mission and lineage would be; what tribe He would come from; what His name would be; how He was going to be mistreated by His own people; that He would be called a Nazarene; that He would speak in parables, and many other details about Him, why didn't these "experts" in Jewish Law and Scripture recognize Him when He finally came to Earth? What more information could they possibly have needed and wanted that wasn't given to them by the Prophets, and even by Jesus Christ Himself – in Person? This kept going through my mind.

One day, I opened the Bible and read: "And as they were coming down the mountain, he [Jesus] charged them to tell no one what they had seen, until the Son of man should have risen from the dead. So they kept the matter to themselves, questioning what the rising from the dead meant" (Mk 9:9-10). I then turned a few pages and read: "And Jesus went on with his disciples, to the villages of Caesare'a Philip'pi; and on the way he asked his disciples, 'Who do men say that I am?' And they told him, 'John the Baptist; and others say, Eli'jah; and others one of the prophets.' And he asked them, 'But who do you say that I am?' Peter answered him, 'You are the Christ.' And he charged them to tell no one about him' " (8:27-30). First, "tell no one what they had seen," and then, "tell no one about him"? I asked myself, "Why the secrecy"?

These curiosities became a research project and the answers revealed not only why the Jewish experts did not recognize

Jesus as the foretold Messiah, but also a little about "the secrecy" and how Jesus prepared for His Sacrificial Mission; even perhaps the steps God took in order to ensure its success. This led to the writing of the present booklet: "Who Do *You* Say I Am?" which eventually became Chapter 7 of a larger work entitled: "A Race Redeemed." This larger work briefly explains the origin of the Universe and how planet Earth came to be, the creation of the first human beings, how their relationship with God was broken by their sin leading to evil, illness, suffering, and death, how – and why – God prepared a savior to restore this broken relationship, **why this Savior was not recognized when He finally came**, and how this Restoration resulted in the formation of a brand new religion: a "Catholic" ("Universal") religion, established by none other than God Himself in Person. The larger work gives a more complete picture to the reader about the **real** world we live in; a sort of "sketch of existence" in order to arrive at some level of understanding of the reality all of us are in.

The researching and writing of this booklet, as well as the larger work, has brought me much closer to Our Tender Father in Heaven; to our Lord Jesus Christ, our brother, Redeemer, and God; to the Holy Spirit, our Helper and Counselor; and to our sweet Blessed Mother, Mediatrix of all Graces, mother of Jesus and tender mother of us all. And last but not least, to a fuller appreciation of the Work God has done for all mankind through Christ, our Lord; an appreciation that continues to grow.

Juan Novo

Chapter 1

"And as they were coming down the mountain, Jesus commanded them, 'Tell no one the vision, until the Son of man is raised from the dead' " (Mt 17:9).

THE "SPARK"

For some strange reason, the above passage from Matthew's Gospel took me completely by surprise one fine day while reading Scripture. Even though I had read and heard that same passage countless times, this time it struck me totally different. The words acted like a spark thrown into a pile of dry kindling and my curiosity was set on fire. "Tell no one the vision? Why the secrecy?" I asked myself. I began to search through all four Gospels to see how many similar passages I could find and was surprised at what I found. Further research led to the discovery that the term "Messianic Secret" had been created to identify the New Testament (NT) passages where Jesus forbids the disclosure of His healings, exorcisms, miracles, and supernatural incidents, and eventually, His true identity. This was truly fascinating! I had never heard of this before! And I again wondered, "Why the secrecy?"

The parallel to Matthew's passage quoted above in Mark's Gospel is: "And as they were coming down the mountain, he charged them to tell no one what they had seen, until the Son of man should have risen from the dead. So they kept the matter to themselves, questioning what the rising from the dead meant" (Mk 9:9-10). Even more mystery! After reading this, the thought occurred to me, "What or who was responsible for making sure that nothing and no one would interfere with and/or prevent the death of Christ in order to make Redemption a successful reality?" I agree this may sound like a silly question, but it really isn't. For surely, if the Pharisees, Sadducees, and the crowd yelling at Pilate to crucify Jesus actually knew and believed that Jesus was the foretold Messiah, and moreover, the Son of God, God in the flesh, they certainly, of course, would not have demanded His execution, and consequently, the Redemption of mankind would not have taken place.[1] Would I even be here, writing this today? Therefore, and it is a very interesting question, "What and/or who kept the Pharisees, scribes and chief priests from realizing and believing that Jesus was indeed the prophesied Messiah, the Son of the Living God?"

This brought me back to the initial question, "Why did Jesus want to keep His divinity a secret?" That question kept running through my mind, over and over again. I thought, "There must be a very good reason for this. Jesus always had – and has – a very good reason and purpose for everything He says and does." The word "Christ" is not a name at all but a title. It is derived from the Greek word "christos" which is a translation of the Hebrew word "meshiah" (Messiah), "the Anointed One." The meanings of the words "Messiah" and "Christ" eventually became one and the same. This explains why we find the expression in the NT "Jesus the Christ," which means "Jesus the Messiah." There are prophecies in the Old Testament (OT) that describe the expected Messiah or Christ as the "Son of God," and also, the "Son of man." However, the Catholic Encyclopedia states that in the time of Christ, the term Son of man was not widely known as a Messianic title.[2]

As I continued my research, I discovered much to my surprise that the Jews never had a doctrine of Original Sin (OS) and still don't to this day! I was literally shocked by this surprising fact. According to The Jewish Virtual Library: "The doctrine of original sin is totally unacceptable to Jews. [S]in is an act, not a state of being" [3] (contrary to CCC, 404). So naturally, from the Jewish point of view, there was no need for someone like Jesus: a Messiah from Heaven, i.e., a "Heavenly Messiah," to come to Earth in order to redeem the human race from OS. No OS means no Redeemer is needed and therefore no reason for Jesus to have died on the Cross. This is why Jews and all who practice Judaism still believe that Jesus died for no valid reason.

I believe the lack of this crucial doctrine must have contributed, perhaps to a great degree, to the misinterpretation of the Messianic prophecies contained in the OT by the Pharisees, Essenes, and the general populace, making them think that these pointed to what I call an "Earthly messiah": a mighty warrior from the line of King David who would come one day to free the Jews from servitude and protect them from their enemies (cf. Ps 17), instead of the actual promised "Heavenly Messiah," Jesus, who was coming to redeem the entire human race. The belief in an Earthly messiah who would free the Jews from servitude and bring them secular peace and prosperity, and herald an era of world peace was an official teaching of either the Pharisees or the Essenes. This belief did not come from the scribes: they basically taught the Torah to the people; and not from the Sadducees: they cared not for the Prophets and their messianic prophecies. Although this belief still exists in modern Rabbinic Judaism, which is based on Pharisaic teachings, it may have originated in the Essene community. The Essenes were more devout than the Pharisees. However, according to the Jewish Virtual Library: "The most important of the three [religious groups] were [and are] the Pharisees because they are the spiritual fathers of modern Judaism." [4] (Evidently, the Essenes are not considered as important to modern Jews.)

6

Logic dictates that the absence of a doctrine of Original Sin in Judaism would account, and perhaps mainly, for why the Jews were not — and still are not — expecting a Heavenly Messiah; this being the root cause. Add to this the fact that since the Jews were ignorant of the Holy Trinity, that there existed more than one Divine Person, it was truly and completely inconceivable to them that God the Father would send His only begotten Son to Earth one day, assume a human body, and walk side by side with them like an ordinary person. So, adding these together, it is not surprising to see why Jesus was found guilty of blasphemy when after His arrest He told the High Priest the truth: that He indeed was God. To the Sadducees, Pharisees, Essenes, and scribes, the "experts" in religion, this was the most serious crime of all, a crime punishable only by death, but this death, interestingly enough, would ensure the Redemption of the entire human race! What a mystery!

Evidenced by the above passages from Matthew and Mark, since Jesus kept telling his followers and also those He cured not to tell anyone who He was and who had cured them, did this "cloak of secrecy" contribute to or further the ignorance of His divinity on the part of the Pharisees, the chief priests, the Essenes, and the teachers of the Law? The answer would seem to be "Yes." Even though Jesus performed supernatural miracles impossible for a human to perform: curing the born blind and mute, raising the dead, instantly curing leprosy and physical deformities, casting out demons, etc., the "conditioned" minds of the Pharisees, Sadducees, and others were not able to realize this was God in the flesh. (More on this "conditioning" in chapter 4.) In fact, they attributed His power to perform these miracles to Satan and not to God (Mt 12:24).

As I mentioned earlier, this very unique "phenomena" became known after the Resurrection of Christ as the

Messianic Secret (MS), and it was the MS, together with the Three Contributing Factors (TCF) listed in the next chapter, that were – and still are – largely responsible for the ignorance the Jews had – and still have – about Jesus Christ being the foretold Heavenly Messiah: the Son of the Living God in the flesh. Let's take a look at these Factors.

Chapter 2

THE EVIDENCE

The Three Contributing Factors

1. No Doctrine of Original Sin.
2. Because of 1, no reason for - or expectancy of - a Redeemer. (Led to the misinterpretation of Messianic prophecies).
3. No Doctrine of the Holy Trinity.

The fact that the Jews did not have a doctrine of Original Sin and were therefore not expecting a Heavenly Messiah to redeem the human race from this Sin and all other sins, and much less, that the Messiah was going to be God in the flesh, facilitated the concealment of Christ's divine identity which was aided by implementing the "policy of secrecy" (MS) in order to secure and bring His redemptive Sacrifice on the Cross for the eternal benefit of mankind to certain completion.

In short, the TCF combined with the MS explains fully why the Jews did not accept Christ as the Heavenly Messiah that He was then and still is now. Some may say, "But what about Peter, Nathanael, and Simeon? They called Jesus the Son of God and Messiah. What about them?" One must remember that in the case of Peter, his declaration was a revelation given to him by the Father (Mt 16:17); he did not come to that conclusion on his own – and he still denied knowing Jesus three (3) times!

In the case of Simeon and Nathanael, and don't forget Anna, the NT says that Simeon was "righteous and devout.... and the Holy Spirit was upon him. And it had been revealed to him by the Holy Spirit that he should not see death before he had seen the Lord's Christ" (Lk 2:25-26). So Simeon, inspired by the Holy Spirit, was indeed expecting the Heavenly Messiah, for God reveals truth to the poor in spirit. In the case of Nathanael, and for that matter, Philip, who told Nathanael, "We have found him of whom Moses in the law and also the prophets wrote, Jesus of Nazareth, the son of Joseph" (Jn 1:45), it just may be that they too, like Simeon, were inspired by the Holy Spirit. On the other hand however, perhaps they thought Jesus was the expected Earthly messiah. It is difficult to tell for certain.

Now in the case of the prophetess Anna, the NT says: "And coming up at that very hour she gave thanks to God, and spoke of him [the child] to all who were looking for the redemption of Jerusalem" (Lk 2:38). Although some say that this places Anna in the same category as Simeon expecting the Heavenly Messiah, and this may indeed be the case, mentioning that she spoke of the child to "all who were looking for the **redemption of Jerusalem**" can also be construed to mean she considered the child to be the Earthly messiah expected to free Jerusalem from Roman rule. On the other hand, it can also mean that she told those who were expecting an Earthly messiah that the child was in fact the Heavenly Messiah instead, the One they were not expecting. God only knows for sure, but the Church teaches that Anna was indeed inspired by the Holy Spirit. Nevertheless, these examples here are very isolated cases, for the majority of the Jews, including the Pharisees, Essenes, Sadducees, Elders, and the teachers of the Law, were eagerly expecting an Earthly messiah, of that there is no doubt whatsoever, and the official Jewish record is very clear on this.[5]

On many occasions (not all are recorded in Scripture), Jesus told His followers, as well as those He cured, not to tell anyone who He was or who cured them. And moreover, He also told them not to mention to anyone certain miracles He had performed, including supernatural events they had witnessed in His presence (Mk 1:44, 5:43, 7:36, 8:30, 9:9; Mt 16:20; 17:9). Jesus even commanded the demons – more than once – not to say who He was! (Mk 1:34; 3:12.) One excellent explanation of this is found in the "Catena Aurea" by St. Thomas Aquinas: "Furthermore, the reason that He forbade the devils to speak, was to teach us not to believe them, even if they say true. For if once they find persons to believe them, they mingle truth with falsehood." [6] This technique of mingling truth with lies (half-truths) was fathered by Satan himself and was first used on Eve in the Garden of Eden with Catastrophic results.

Although Jesus told many of those He cured not to say anything to anyone about the cures, many of these did not listen to Him and spread the news everywhere. Here are some examples:

Evidence Of Secrecy

MATTHEW: "When he entered the house, the blind men came to him; and Jesus said to them, 'Do you believe that I am able to do this?' They said to him, 'Yes, Lord.' Then he touched their eyes, saying, 'According to your faith let it be done to you.' And their eyes were opened. And Jesus sternly charged them, 'See that no one knows it.' But they went away and spread his fame through all that district" (9:28-31).

"He said to them, 'But who do you say that I am?' Simon Peter replied, 'You are the Christ, the Son of the living God'…. Then he strictly charged the disciples to tell no one that he was the Christ" (16:15-16, 20; cf. 12:16).

After Jesus' Transfiguration up on a high mountain, where Moses and Elijah talked with Jesus, "And as they were coming down the mountain, Jesus commanded them, 'Tell no one the vision, until the Son of man is raised from the dead' " (17:9).

MARK: "And immediately there was in their synagogue a man with an unclean spirit; and he cried out, 'What have you to do with us, Jesus of Nazareth? Have you come to destroy us? I know who you are, the Holy One of God.' But Jesus rebuked him, saying, 'Be silent, and come out of him!' And the unclean spirit, convulsing him and crying with a loud voice, came out of him. And they were all amazed, so that they questioned among themselves, saying, 'What is this? A new teaching! With authority he commands even the unclean spirits, and they obey him.' And at once his fame spread everywhere throughout all the surrounding region of Galilee" (1:23-28).

"That evening, at sundown, they brought to him all who were sick or possessed with demons. And the whole city was gathered together about the door. And he healed many who were sick with various diseases, and cast out many demons; and he would not permit the demons to speak, because they knew him" (1:32-34).

"And a leper came to him begging him, and kneeling said to him, 'If you will, you can make me clean.' Moved with pity, he stretched out his hand and touched him, and said to him, 'I will; be clean.' And immediately the leprosy left him, and he was made clean. And he sternly charged him, and sent him away at once, and said to him, 'See that you say nothing to any one; but go, show yourself to the priest, and offer for your cleansing what Moses commanded, for a proof to the people.' But he went out and began to talk freely about it, and to spread the news, so that Jesus could no longer openly enter a town, but was out in the country; and people came to him from every quarter" (1:40-45).

"And they brought to him a man who was deaf and had an impediment in his speech; and they begged him to lay his hand upon him. And taking him aside from the multitude privately, he put his fingers into his ears, and he spat and touched his tongue; and looking up to heaven, he sighed, and said to him, 'Eph'phatha,' that is, 'Be opened.' And his ears were opened, his tongue was released, and he spoke plainly. And he charged them to tell no one; but the more he charged them, the more zealously they proclaimed it. And they were astonished beyond measure, saying, 'He has done all things well; he even makes the deaf hear and the mute speak' " (7:32-37).

"And Jesus went on with his disciples, to the villages of Caesare'a Philip'pi; and on the way he asked his disciples, 'Who do men say that I am?' And they told him, 'John the Baptist; and others say, Eli'jah; and others one of the prophets.' And he asked them, 'But who do you say that I am?' Peter answered him, 'You are the Christ.' And he charged them to tell no one about him" (8:27-30).

Similar to the passage in Matthew's Gospel, after Jesus' Transfiguration we find: "And as they were coming down the mountain, he charged them to tell no one what they had seen, until the Son of man should have risen from the dead. So they kept the matter to themselves, questioning what the rising from the dead meant" (9:9-10).

LUKE: "Now when the sun was setting, all those who had any that were sick with various diseases brought them to him; and he laid his hands on every one of them and healed them. And demons also came out of many, crying, 'You are the Son of God!' But he rebuked them, and would not

13

allow them to speak, because they knew that he was the Christ" (4:40-41).

"While he was in one of the cities, there came a man full of leprosy; and when he saw Jesus, he fell on his face and begged him, 'Lord, if you will, you can make me clean.' And he stretched out his hand, and touched him, saying, 'I will; be clean.' And immediately the leprosy left him. And he charged him to tell no one; but 'go and show yourself to the priest, and make an offering for your cleansing, as Moses commanded, for a proof to the people.' But so much the more the report went abroad concerning him; and great multitudes gathered to hear and to be healed of their infirmities. But he withdrew to the wilderness and prayed" (5:12-16).

"And when he came to the house, he permitted no one to enter with him, except Peter and John and James, and the father and mother of the child. And all were weeping and bewailing her; but he said, 'Do not weep; for she is not dead but sleeping.' And they laughed at him, knowing that she was dead. But taking her by the hand he called, saying, 'Child, arise.' And her spirit returned, and she got up at once; and he directed that something should be given her to eat. And her parents were amazed; but he charged them to tell no one what had happened" (8:51-56).

JOHN: Interestingly enough, I did not find a single example of the Messianic Secret in John's Gospel, only in the Synoptics.

So again, the question is, "Why the secrecy?" Why did Jesus command His followers and even the demons not to tell anyone who He really was? In fact, you would think that the opposite would have been the case; i.e., that Christ would have wanted everyone to know who He was, that the

14

True promised Messiah had finally come, and moreover, that He was also God's Son: God in the flesh. This would have corrected the false "Earthly messiah" notions that most of them had and adhered to. But that is not what happened; that was not what Jesus wanted. Why not?

Some of the early Church Fathers believed that Jesus told some of those He cured not to say anything about the incidents because He wanted to teach His followers the value of humility, to avoid vainglory, showiness, and not to profit from the Good News they were going to preach and the miracles they would perform themselves, and yet other Church Fathers believed that Jesus was indeed trying to keep His divinity a secret in order to eliminate obstructions and impediments to the Redemption of mankind through His sacrificial death on the Cross.

Let's take a look at the Patristic evidence on this and see what the early Church Fathers had to say in this regard. The following excerpts are taken from St. Thomas Aquinas' "Catena Aurea" (CA).

Chapter 3

SOME EXAMPLES

Examples Against Vainglory/Profit

On Mt 8:1-4: The curing of a leper: "Jesus when healing his body bids him tell no man; *Jesus saith unto him, See thou tell no man.* Some say that He gave this command that they might not through malice distrust his cure. But this is said foolishly, for He did not so cure him as that his purity should be called in question; but He bids him tell no man, to teach that He does not love ostentation and glory. How is it then that to another to whom He had healed He gives command to go and tell it? [Mk 5:19] What He taught in that was only that we should have a thankful heart; for He does not command that it should be published abroad, but that glory should be given to God. He teaches us then through this leper **not to be desirous of empty honour;** by the other, not to be ungrateful, but to refer all things to the praise of God." (CA, Vol. I, St. Mt., Part 1, p. 300. Chrys.) [My emph.]

On Mk 1:40-45: The curing of a leper: "As if He said, It is not yet time that My works should be preached, I require not thy preaching. By which He teaches us **not to seek worldly honour** as a reward for our works." (CA, Vol. 1I, St. Mark, p. 34. Chrys..) [My emph.]

On Lk 5:12-14: The curing of a leper: "*And he commanded him that he should tell it to no one,* that in truth he might teach us that our good deeds are not to be made public, but to be rather concealed, that **we should abstain not only from gaining money, but even favour**" (CA, Luke, p. 182. Ambrose.) [My emph.]

16

On Lk 5:12-14: The curing of a leper: "And although the Lord in giving out remedies advised telling them to no one, **instructing us to avoid pride**." (CA, Luke, p.183. Chrys.) [My emph.]

Examples On Secrecy Of Divinity

On Lk 4:41: The declaration of demons: "The devils confess the Son of God, and as it is afterwards said, 'they knew him to be Christ'; for when the devil saw Him distressed by fasting [in the desert], he perceived Him to be truly man, but when he prevailed not in his trial [with Pilate] he doubted whether or not He were the Son of God, but now by the power of Christ's miracles he either perceived or suspected Him to be the Son of God. He [Satan] did not then persuade the Jews to crucify Him because he thought Him not to be Christ or the Son of God, but because he did not foresee that by this death he himself would be condemned. Of this mystery hidden from the world the Apostle says, that none of the princes of this world knew, **for if they had known** [His divinity] **they would never have crucified the Lord of Glory**." (CA, Luke, p. 169. Bede; cf. 1 Cor 7-8.) [My emph.]

On Lk 4:41: "But the Apostles themselves are commanded to be silent concerning Him, lest by proclaiming His divine Majesty, **the dispensation of His Passion should be delayed**." (CA, Luke, p. 170. Bede; cf. 1 Cor 2:6-9.) [My emph.]

On Mk 1:32-34: The declaration of demons: "For the devils knew that He was the Christ, who had been promised by the Law: for they saw in Him all the signs, which had been foretold by the Prophets; **but they** [the Jews] **were ignorant of His divinity**, as also were 'their princes,' **for if they had known it, they would not have crucified the**

17

Lord of glory." (CA, Vol II, St. Mark, p. 29-30. Pseudo-Aug.) [My emph.]

On Mt 17:9: After the Transfiguration: "**Or, because if His majesty should be published among the people, they should hinder the dispensation of His passion, by resistance to the chief Priests; and thus the redemption of the human race should suffer impediment**" (CA, Vol I, St. Mt., Part 1, p. 607. Remigius.) [My emph.]

In this last passage, St. Remigius believes that if Christ's divinity had been regularly divulged, disseminated and spread widely throughout the land, the people would have learned that Jesus was indeed God in the flesh, the True and Heavenly Messiah, and therefore would have prevented the Pharisees and Sadducees from demanding His execution before Pilate and the Redemption of the human race would not have taken place.

An email reply I received from Father George W. Rutler in this regard contained the following:

"The explanation of Saint Remigius became the standard way of dealing with the so-called Messianic secret although it was considered more often in recent times than traditionally by the fathers."

Although St. Remigius, who lived from 437-533 AD, is not considered a Father of the Church (even though the middle of the eighth century is generally regarded as the close of the age of the Fathers), St. Gregory of Tours refers to Remigius as "a man of great learning, fond of rhetorical studies, and equal in his holiness to St. Silvester." [7] Moreover, St. Thomas Aquinas considered his beliefs important enough to include them throughout his Catena Aurea.

18

The above four examples have considerable weight in showing that Jesus most likely wanted to keep His real identity a secret, at least for as long as possible, so that the Pharisees, Essenes and Sadducees (chief priests) would not come to realize He was indeed the Son of God and therefore see Him as a blasphemer that needed to be put to death when He claimed that title. This perspective cannot be ignored or dismissed in light of the evidence thus presented.

In light of the above, I believe the MS had at least two (if not more) objectives and purposes:

1. Teach His followers the virtues of humility against vainglory, pride, and worldly profit;

2. Conceal His divine identity.

This "Policy of Secrecy" (MS) surely contributed to making His Redemptive Sacrificial Mission a guaranteed success. To what degree? It is hard to say. St. Mark's account stated earlier of the Transfiguration (9:9) strongly supports this point of view: "And as they were coming down the mountain, he charged them to tell no one what they had seen, until the Son of man should have risen from the dead."

QUESTION: Why were they ordered not to reveal His identity until **after** the Resurrection?

ANSWER: To ensure the arrest, condemnation and crucifixion in order to redeem mankind.

There doesn't seem to be a more logical answer. It was not Christ's Resurrection that redeemed mankind, but His Crucifixion and Death. This is why Catholics have

Crucifixes with the Corpus of Christ on it in churches, rosaries, holy cards, hanging on walls, etc. : to remind us of our Redemption. Protestants do not have this. I remember at work one day, a Protestant lady said to me, "You Catholics still have Jesus on the cross!" My reply: "A Reminder of our Redemption."

If the Pharisees, Essenes and chief priests had come to believe that Christ was the Son of God, they certainly would never have harmed a single hair on His head! But as we all know, that's not what actually happened, and we have God to thank for that Blessed Sacrifice He endured for our sake.

Here's another thing to think about. If the prophets had been completely explicit and included in their prophecies that the promised Messiah was going to be God Himself in the flesh, would come in a human body, and their instructions were to execute Him in order to redeem the human race, do you really think they would have done such a thing? Arrest a person who they knew for sure was God Himself, and then consent to have Him tortured and have huge nails driven through His hands and feet to a tree? And then mock Him, strike Him, make fun of Him, and watch Him die a horrible death? Are you mad? Kill God? And be responsible and guilty for such a heinous and abominable crime, and then be sent to Hell for all Eternity for doing so? Personally, I really don't think so. In fact, if the Prophets had given them explicit instructions to kill the Son of God, the Jews certainly would have had good reason for stoning them to death!

It therefore appears that the reality of the Trinity: three divine Persons in one Godhead, was not revealed by God to the Jews in OT times perhaps for a very intentional and specific reason: to put it simply, so that the Jews would believe that there *is* only one God, only one Divine Person, and this would be very helpful in aiding Jesus to conceal His real identity when He embarked on His public ministry – miracles included. The solitary "oneness" of God was hammered into the Jewish mind so often and so effectively that no one suspected there could have been more than one Divine Person, and much less, that He would send His Son as Messiah to redeem humanity. Let's take a close look at why the Jews did not have a doctrine of the Holy Trinity.

Chapter 4

THE
"MORE THAN ONE GOD"
JEWISH PROBLEM

The MAIN problem the Jews had in believing that Jesus was the Son of God, in particular the Sadducees, Essenes, Pharisees, and scribes, is that since childhood, they, and all Jewish children, were explicitly taught that there was only one God: one Almighty Person who was God, the Creator of all things. The prayer that all Jewish children learn to memorize (and therefore internalize) regarding the monotheistic oneness of God is the "Shema Yisrael," and the very first verse of this prayer is:

"Hear, O Israel: The Lord our God, the Lord is ONE." (Mk 12:29; cf. Dt 6:4.)

Thus, to all Jews, "the Lord is ONE" meant (and means) "There is only ONE God," not two, or three, or a hundred. This monotheistic oneness of God was extremely important to the Jewish people because other surrounding ethnic cultures, including the Romans who ruled them during Christ's time, were polytheistic believing in and worshipping many gods, pagan gods made of stone, clay, gold, and other things, who obviously had nothing to do with the creation of the universe. As a matter of fact, the first of the Ten Commandments given to the Jews through Moses at Mt. Sinai is:

"I am the Lord thy god, who brought thee out of the land of Egypt, out of the house of bondage."

Therefore, for someone to come along and say that *he* is the Son of God, meaning he too is God, which is precisely what Jesus eventually did, was the greatest and worse form of blasphemy that could have entered the ear of any Jew, especially the ear of a Pharisee or chief priest, for that would mean that there is more than just one God. This would be diametrically opposed to what they had been taught all their lives, and taught to them by God Himself! Such a statement, coming from another human being, which is what Jesus was to the Pharisees and Sadducees, was the greatest and worse form of blasphemy possible, punishable only by death. Since this is what Jesus in fact did after He was arrested and taken to the house of Cai'aphas, the High Priest of the Jews, the capital punishment of crucifixion was the only and proper way to punish this terrible crime. And since the Jews under Roman rule were not allowed to execute anyone, for that "authority" was reserved only to the Romans, the Pharisees, Sadducees, and teachers of the Law (scribes) demanded that Jesus be crucified, and after much debate back and forth, the cruel and unjust act was carried out.

A very important clarification needs to be made here. The concept and reality of the Holy Trinity: the Father, the Son, and the Holy Spirit, was not known to the Jews prior to the arrival of Christ. No one on Earth knew about this sacred mystery. It was Jesus Himself who taught His Apostles this mysterious and profound reality, and He started by introducing the Father to them, talking about Him; how He and the Father were one, for example (Jn 10:30); and that His Father's house (Temple) was not a marketplace (Jn 2:16); and when the Jews persecuted Him for healing on the Sabbath, He replied: "My Father is working still, and I am working" (Jn 5:17). The Gospels reveal that Jesus went off by Himself to pray to the Father many times during His public ministry, and I am sure many times even before that.

Sometimes Jesus would pray to the Father early in the morning when no one else was up yet (Mk 1:35), and at other times during the entire night (Lk 6:12). And then there's the time when Jesus taught His disciples how to pray to *our* Father, now known as the Lord's Prayer and the Our Father Prayer (Mt 6:9).

Although the Gospels show Jesus mentioning the Holy Spirit here and there, it was toward the end of His ministry, as His Passion drew near, that He spoke to His Apostles at length about the Holy Spirit, third Person of the Trinity, calling Him the "Helper," the "Counselor": "I have yet many things to say to you, but you cannot bear them now. When the Spirit of truth comes, **he** will guide you into all the truth; for **he** will not speak on **his** own authority, but whatever **he** hears **he** will speak, and **he** will declare to you the things that are to come. **He** will glorify me, for **he** will take what is mine and declare it to you. All that the Father has is mine; therefore I said that **he** will take what is mine and declare it to you" (Jn 16:12-15) [my emph.]. All this, together with what He revealed to them after His Resurrection, completed the teaching of the Holy Trinity, a teaching that although grew clearer and clearer as time marched on, is still a great mystery to this day. Incidentally, Theophilus of Antioch is credited with being the first to use the word "Trinity" in describing the Triune God.

I'll never forget, one time I was out doing yard work and some Jehovah's Witnesses came up to me and started talking about the Bible. I used to tell them I was Catholic, was very happy to be so, and they would walk away, but this time I continued the conversation which led to them mentioning the Holy Spirit not being a person but only a force or power that one can get by being close to God. This was too much of a temptation for me, so I told them to wait and went and got my Bible. At that point in my life, I did not know where to look in the Bible for evidence on this topic, so I just opened it, and miraculously, it opened to John's Gospel, Chapter 14. I read verses 15-17, 25-26, and then skipped to 16:12-15 (quoted above), where the Spirit is repeatedly referred to as "he" and "his." I then said to them, "So you see, if the Spirit is only a force or power, why does the Bible call the Spirit 'he' and 'his'?" The two elders looked at each other and didn't say anything, but the two younger ones were really excited and interested in what I said, but before I could say anything else, the two elders took the young ones by the arms and led them away saying their farewells. I waved back and said, "Have a nice day! Come back anytime. I have some very good videos on Jehovah's Witnesses that you'll like!" I never saw them again, but I prayed for them!

Nature And Person

In order to get some understanding of the doctrine of the Holy Trinity, we must first understand the difference and relationship between nature and person. In his outstanding book, "Theology and Sanity," Frank Sheed explains this topic very well. I will try my best to synthesize it here. God the Father is not God the Son, and God the Son is not God the Holy Spirit, and God the Holy Spirit is not God the Father. Yet, the Father is God, the Son is God, and the Holy Spirit is also God, but there are not three Gods, only One. The key to understanding here is in the words "person" and "nature." There is no arithmetical miracle here where three equals one somehow; or that three persons are stuffed into one person; none of that. To say, for example, that I possess a human nature automatically means that I am a person. I would certainly not be a human person if I did not possess a human nature, but it is me, the person, who possesses that human nature, not the other way around! Therefore, the word "nature" describes "what" I am, and the word

25

"person" describes "who" I am. Every living being has a nature but not all beings are persons. If you are startled by something moving in the bushes at night, you'll probably say, "What is that?" And if a cat walks out, you'll say, "Oh, it's just a cat!" But if you suddenly see instead a profile of a man, you wouldn't say "What is that?" but rather "Who is that?" What refers to the nature of the being and who refers to the person. On Earth, only rational human beings are persons; nothing else is. If you called a rock or a potato a person, people would look at you funny!

Nature says what we are and also what we can and can't do. Human nature allows us to walk, run, jump, think, laugh, love, cry, sleep, and many other wonderful things, but a snake can only do one of these – sleep; and a rock can do none of them. Bird nature allows it to walk, swim, and fly, yet we humans can do the first two but not the last one (although we can now fly in a plane). And fish nature allows a fish to naturally live underwater which we naturally can't do (cf. 1 Cor. 15:39). Although it is the nature that determines what operations are possible for us to do, it is we, the persons, who do them. So, although one might be tempted to think that there are two distinct realities co-existing in every human: the what (nature) and the who (person), or perhaps two levels of only one reality, we cannot see clearly enough into our souls to be totally sure.

It is truly baffling to ponder the actual mystery of our existence. The only person who truly knows us very well is ourselves; i.e., no one knows you better than you do, right? Yet, if you look into your soul, your "self," and try to see what is the distinction between the what and the who in you, it is not a clear picture at all, but rather a veiled one. If someone asked you, "Tell me about yourself," for example, "but leave out all of the qualities you have, your name, where you were born and raised, and all the things you have ever done in life, only tell me about the self that possesses those qualities and has done all those things," you would not be able to tell that person anything about your "self." You know, of course, that there is something, someone there, but it is out of focus, you can't get a good glimpse of it; it's as if the soul does not want to be looked at!

Three Divine Persons – One Nature

Although we can't see that deep into our selves enough to make out the distinction between our human nature and our personhood, we can at least see that only one nature can be possessed and operated by only one person. But the concept that one nature can be totally possessed and operated – at one and the same time – by three distinct Persons is difficult to see and understand. It isn't difficult to accept it as true, but it is difficult in seeing what it means. It is very important to note that the three distinct Persons of the Trinity are not three separate Persons, only three distinct Persons because they can't be separated since each one totally possesses the one same divine nature. And they don't "share" this nature; each one totally possesses it in its entirety. As I mentioned earlier, since the nature says what we are and what we can and can't do, each Person is God, wholly and equally with the other two, and each one can do everything that the divine nature allows them to do: to be God. The one unique quality of the Oneness of God, the oneness of divine nature, is that all three Persons have only one Will and only one Intellect because there is only one nature. Unlike three humans who possess three separate human natures with three separate wills and intellects, which means all three think differently, know differently, love differently, and act differently, all three Divine Persons totally possess only one Will and only one

27

Intellect. Thus, all three Know all things with only One Intellect and all three Love with only One Will. Three Persons, One will, One Intellect, not three Gods. Only One God: Jesus said, "I and the Father are one" (Jn 10:30). The "Oneness" of the Trinity is a profound Mystery.

It is equally important to know that the word "God" is not the Father's name, nor is it Jesus' name, nor is it the name of the Holy Spirit. The word "God" simply refers to the nature, the divine nature, and some of the characteristics or attributes of this utterly perfect divine nature are: Unity, Immutability, Simplicity, Omnipotence, Omniscience, and Omnipresence. We humans, on the other hand, only possess a human nature which does not have any of those qualities. But the Father possesses the divine nature, Jesus, the Son, possesses both the divine nature and also a human nature, and the Holy Spirit possesses the divine nature. They don't share the divine nature. They each possess it entirely. Although all three Persons possess the divine nature, there are not three Gods but only one God: one nature. Thus, there *is* only ONE God! [8]

When we Catholics say there is only one God, much the same as when the Jews say there is only one God, both of us, in actuality, are right, because there is in fact only one divine nature, which is what the word "God" refers to. But that divine nature, unbeknownst to the Jews, which included the Pharisees, Essenes, Sadducees, Elders, and scribes (teachers of the Law) is totally and completely possessed by three distinct Persons: the Holy Trinity: a deep and profound mystery that has been taught and handed down from generation to generation by the Holy Roman Catholic Church: the One, Holy, Catholic, and Apostolic Church founded by Jesus Christ (God) over 2000 years ago. The doctrine of the Trinity is something the Jews were not taught and therefore were ignorant of. It does not appear anywhere in the OT, nor in the Hebrew Bible, the Talmud, or in any other Jewish publication or written record to date, but Jesus taught it to His Jewish disciples. The doctrine of the Holy Trinity is a very profound mystery. We humans will never totally come to understand it fully, but that's ok! We don't need to. But we should look forward to one day being able to enjoy the utter bliss of gazing upon Them in Person for all Eternity. Without Time.

"Now surely I do see what an immense effect such a doctrine [of the Holy Trinity] must have upon life. It is no mere question for theologians, but one that concerns every living soul. Whatever is allowed by God's power must be guided by His wisdom and urged on by His love. All that happens to me in life, the little worries and the great anxieties, the crises and the daily annoyances, the sorrows and the joys, the harms that reach me through the sins of others, the great crimes of history, the huge and devastating wars, the partings and loves and the whole cycle of human experience are permitted by Power, which is itself wise and loving. These three Persons determine my life, and, since I walk by faith, I must surely grow very patient in my attitude toward life. For how can I complain or criticize God's Providence, since it all comes under that triple influence of Power, Wisdom, and Love? Under the guidance, then, of this mystery, I can walk through the valley of death or the more perilous borders of sin without loss of courage or hopefulness. Nothing can make me afraid. How these are separate, yet one, I do not know, nor can I reconcile in my concrete experience the claims of each. It is always a mystery, but a mystery in which I believe. Whatever Power allows on earth is designed in Wisdom and attuned by Love." (Fr. Bede Jarrett.)

Only faith will bring a person to believe in the Trinity. Reason alone will not suffice. [9]

Even though Jesus performed many miracles: brought to life many from the dead, expelled countless demons from tormented people, cured instantly many illnesses and deformities, and many others, this still did not make the Pharisees, Essenes and chief priests realize that He was God in person, and in fact, they believed quite the opposite: that the devil was giving Him this power: "But when the Pharisees heard it, they said, 'It is only by Be-el'zebul, the prince of demons, that this man casts out demons' " (Mt 12:24).

Since God is "outside of time" and therefore transcends time, this means God knows every single thing that has taken place in human history from its beginning to its end, and this, of course, includes the necessity of Christ's Crucifixion in order to redeem the entire human race. With this in mind, in order to guarantee that the Crucifixion of our Lord would take place at the proper time at the end of His Public Ministry without interruptions of any kind, it seems that God would have had to take certain measures – in advance – to ensure the success of a Mission as important as this one; a success that, needless to say, is extremely important for the eternal benefit of mankind. In this regard, let's take a look at some important measures that God perhaps took to ensure the completion of Christ's Salvific Mission.

Chapter 5

IMPORTANT MEASURES

1. God did not reveal the doctrine of Original Sin and the explicitness of the need for its Redemption to the Hebrews, the Israelites, or the Jews.

2. God did not give explicit descriptions and detailed information about Jesus as the Messiah to the Hebrews, the Israelites, or the Jews through their Prophets. Isaiah is the only Prophet who gives the most details and clues about Christ in his prophecies. The other prophecies only give vague and cryptic descriptions and obscure information about Him so that it wouldn't be obvious to the Jewish authorities and the people that Jesus would be God in the flesh and therefore refuse to have Him executed thereby preventing the redemptive Crucifixion to the detriment of mankind. Although there were enough combined prophetic clues that pointed to a Heavenly Messiah, the scribes, Pharisees, Essenes and Sadducees did not "assemble the pieces" to realize it.

3. God did reveal the oneness of God to them, but withheld the reality of the Holy Trinity which led to the daily repetition of the Shema "Oneness of God" prayer and a rock-hard monotheistic mentality. Thus, by not revealing the mystery of the Trinity in OT times, the possibility of God the Father sending to Earth His only Son, one of the Divine Persons, on a redemptive Mission that would include assuming a human body would never enter the Jewish mind; it would be totally impossible and inconceivable to them.

4. God's Divine Providence directed and ordered the lives of the Jews in a certain way, from inception of adoption as

Chosen People to the coming of the Messiah, that allowed them to undergo severe hardships and suffering from time to time during their history (as punishment for their sins) in order to set their minds firmly on the hopes for an "Earthly messiah" (facilitating the concealment of Christ's divinity) that would come and free them from Gentile domination. Personally, I believe the Pharisees are the ones largely responsible for not only the misinterpretations of the Messianic prophecies, but also for the dissemination of the belief in an Earthly messiah before and during the time of Christ.

5. Last but not least, God had the Messiah expose the hypocrisy, sinfulness, lack of Scripture understanding, and unjust behavior of the Pharisees, chief priests, and teachers of the Law – for all to see – to make them "mad as Hell" at the Christ and give them a good reason for wanting to kill Him thereby securing the Redemptive Sacrifice of "the Lamb of God, who takes away the sin of the world" (Jn 1:29).

There is no doubt that numbers 1 and 2 were certainly put in place by God since Judaism did not have – and still does not have – neither the doctrine of Original Sin nor the doctrine of a Heavenly Messiah: God in the flesh, both of which are still absent from Rabbinic Judaism to this day. Number 3 was also put in place by God for the reason stated therein (also missing from Rabbinic Judaism to this day). Number 4 does not mean that God Himself inflicted hardships and sufferings on the Chosen People, but rather allowed these things to take place at certain times and of certain severities, and not only for their own good (as punishment for sins), but for that of mankind as well, for Scripture says that a Loving God punishes those He loves (Prv 3:12; Heb 12:5-11), and the Gardener prunes his Vine in order for it to produce more fruit (Jn 15:1-2). These, however, appear to be secondary while the primary objective was the consequential effect of these: to expect an Earthly messiah to rescue them. And number 5 seems pretty clear-cut as found in Scripture, for the religious Elite: the Pharisees, chief priests and scribes, had indeed fallen into a hypocritical mindset (Mt 23:13); they believed they were exempt from sinning (Jn 8:7), did not understand some of the Scriptures properly (Mt 22:46), especially the Messianic prophecies, and treated their people unjustly (Mt 23:1-4; 13-15).

At this point it is important to point out that God is the most Tender and Loving Father, with a Love, Mercy and Compassion way beyond our imaginations and understandings. Concrete proof of this was given to us, beyond the shadow of a doubt, by sending His only Beloved Son to suffer a cruel and horrible death for our Eternal benefit, not His. So don't misunderstand me when I said that He allowed terrible things to happen to His Chosen People, because this was not only as punishment for their sinfulness, but also to insure the success of His Son's Mission on Earth for the benefit of all mankind. It really does not take much to realize that God does indeed work in very mysterious ways, but always, always does so from pure Love for us.

This brings to mind an interesting question: "Why did Jesus embark on a life of public ministry that included performing supernatural miracles – for three long years – if He did not want anyone to know who He really was? Wouldn't the continued performance of miracles over a span of three long years lead others to think He was divine, something He did not want anyone to know? This, at first, does not make sense, for you would think that the last thing He should have done was to perform miracles since it would eventually become obvious that He was not just an ordinary man. But ironically, Jesus had to – and wanted to – perform miracles for several reasons so that His Sacrificial Redemptive Mission **would** be a success. I believe some of the reasons are:

Reasons For Christ's Miracles
(Partial List)

1. The primary reason Jesus exorcised demons from people and healed their diseases is that, now being normal, they could go and worship God in the Temple; they couldn't do that before. Jesus truly loved His people, created in His Image. He wanted to teach them the importance and beauty of Life, the importance and beauty of truth, and wanted to tell them the Good News about the Kingdom of God. He also wanted to cure them because He loved them so much: "As he went ashore he saw a great throng; and he had compassion on them, and healed their sick" (Mt 14:14). "When the crowds learned it, they followed him; and he welcomed them and spoke to them of the kingdom of God, and cured those who had need of healing" (Lk 9:11).

2. Jesus needed His Apostles to believe in Him in order to follow Him and later establish His Church on Earth for the dissemination of the Good News, and this required performing miracles.

"This, the first of his signs, Jesus did at [the wedding in] Cana in Galilee, and manifested his glory; and his disciples believed in him. After this he went down to Caper'na-um, with his mother and his brethren and his disciples; and there they stayed for a few days" (Jn 2:11-12).

3. Jesus conducted Himself in such a way that those who heard Him preach and witnessed the miracles He performed would have no doubt that He was a gifted man of God, a

prophet perhaps, who was sent by God to teach them and help them with their problems and sufferings: "When the chief priests and the Pharisees heard his parables, they perceived that he was speaking about them. But when they tried to arrest him, they feared the multitudes, because they held him to be a prophet" (Mt 21:45-46). Only His Apostles were eventually given the understanding of who He really was, the Son of God, but this became apparent **after** the Resurrection.

4. By performing supernatural miracles, apart from wanting to help His people out of love for them, Jesus would ensure that masses of people would follow Him and believe in Him in order to create a large following; without a large following, He would not have been able to attract attention to Himself, and Jesus needed to attract attention to Himself in order to attract the Pharisees and chief priests who would eventually bring His Sacrificial Mission to sure completion by having Him condemned to death for blasphemy; a Mission that would remain a mystery and a secret until the Last Supper.

The Apostles did not understand – until after the Resurrection, that His Mission was to die for the sins of mankind. Although Jesus told perhaps many of those He cured not to say who cured them, He knew very well that some were going to do just that – it is hard to hold back such good news! Moreover, it is also hard for most people to keep a secret. Jesus knew that too. In some instances, telling secrets results in widespread dissemination, a technique widely used by modern sensational tabloids. Although the miracles themselves would eventually bring large crowds to Him, perhaps Jesus employed this technique selectively to ensure attraction. On the other hand, large crowds would inhibit his ability to move about from town to town, and moreover, too much attention would also attract the authorities – Jewish and/or Roman – and possibly cause a confrontation before the time was right. Nevertheless, Jesus handled everything masterfully. It doesn't appear to be far-fetched to imagine that perhaps during the time Jesus spent in the desert after His Baptism, preparing for His public ministry (Scripture says it was forty days), Jesus began to either formulate a plan, or go over a plan He had already formulated that would ensure the success of His main objective: His Redemptive Death for mankind. It would seem that part of this plan would have to include not revealing to anyone who He was, not until His Mission was coming to an end, for at least a couple of reasons:

Reasons For Secrecy
(Partial List)

1. Revealing His divinity would more than likely frighten people and drive them away instead of attracting them, and as I mentioned earlier, Jesus needed to form a following in order for His Mission to be a success. Fear of God is perhaps a trait in human nature that goes way back – to Adam and Eve!

2. Jesus told some of those He cured (perhaps the majority) not to say anything about the incidents because He wanted to teach His followers the value of humility, to avoid vainglory, showiness, and not to seek profit from the Good News they were going to preach and the miracles they would perform themselves.

3. As I mentioned earlier, His divine nature had to remain a secret to ensure being condemned to death by the Pharisees, chief priests, Elders, and scribes when He revealed this truth to them. St Paul wrote: "But we impart a secret and hidden wisdom of God [the Messiah would be God

36

incarnate], which God decreed before the ages for our glorification. None of the rulers of this age understood this; for if they had, they would not have crucified the Lord of glory" (1 Cor 7-8).

At the very beginning of His ministry, Jesus told Simon and his brother Andrew: "Follow me, and I will make you fishers of men" (Mt 4:18-19), for He was going to teach them, as well as His other Apostles and disciples, how to convert sinners into Christians. However, on the other side of the coin, Jesus was also going to teach his Apostles and disciples how to expose the hypocrisy, the ignorance of Scripture, and the hardness of heart of the Pharisees, chief priests and the scribes so that His followers would not imitate them.

If the Pharisees, Essenes and Sadducees had learned at the start of Jesus' three-year ministry that the long awaited Messiah was God in the flesh and had finally arrived, things would have turned out quite different: surely He would not have been condemned to death by the Jews. On the other hand, if His crucifixion had taken place at the start of His public ministry, Jesus would not have been able to announce the Good News, heal the sick, and expel demons from the possessed as He did during those three years of His ministry, but more important, He would not have had the time to gather and train His Apostles, not only for their missionary work, but also to establish His Church after His Ascension.

If Christ had said to Simon Peter, at the beginning: "Good morning Simon. How are you today?" And Peter had replied: "Very well, thank you sir. And who may I ask are you?" And Christ had said: "I am your Lord and your God." I don't think Peter would have taken this too well. And if Peter had stayed there with his mouth wide open in disbelief after Jesus said this, and Christ had waved His hands to produce thunder and lightning to prove that He indeed was God, I don't think Peter would have stayed around too much longer after that. Do you? It therefore seems logical that a very important part of Jesus' plan was to gradually reveal who He was to His Apostles so as not to scare them away. This, of course, makes perfect sense. Since Jesus had acquired a human body, thanks in no small part to His Holy Mother, Mary (our Mother too), this human body would certainly help to keep His divine identity a secret, for no one would ever suspect that the man called Jesus from Nazareth, the son of Joseph the carpenter, was God. How could Jesus be God since it was obvious He was a human person, like they were? In the Gospel of Matthew, we find a relevant statement that was made by a resident of Nazareth, the town where Jesus was from:

"And when Jesus had finished these parables, he went away from there, and coming to his own country he taught them in their synagogue, so that they were astonished, and said, 'Where did this man get this wisdom and these mighty works? Is not this the carpenter's son? Is not his mother called Mary? And are not his brethren James and Joseph and Simon and Judas? And are not all his sisters with us? Where then did this man get all this?' And they took offense at him. But Jesus said to them, 'A prophet is not without honor except in his own country and in his own house.' And he did not do many mighty works there, because of their unbelief" (Mt 13:53-58).

It is interesting to note here that faith in Jesus almost always resulted in the performance of a miracle for the benefit of the believer, while lack of faith almost always stifled it. The following in this regard is found in the Catena Aurea: "Or he says 'many' because there were some persons, who could not at all be cured on account of their unfaithfulness. Therefore He healed many of those who were brought, that is, all who had faith." [10]

Jesus knew that he was going to be crucified by the Romans at the instigation of the Pharisees and chief priests way in advance; in fact, before the Creation of the Universe. That was the main objective of His mission: willingly sacrifice Himself and lay down His life to redeem mankind. How was He going to make sure they would execute Him? Was He going to commit robbery? Or commit adultery with someone's wife? How about bear false witness against an innocent person? Or perhaps kill someone? No, none of these. God does not commit crimes, and He also does not lie.

So, how was He going to bring about His condemnation so as to be put to death? By telling the truth: that He was the Son of God, the promised Messiah. Even though this was the truth, in the eyes of the Pharisees, Sadducees, and the Elders, this was indeed a crime: a crime punishable by death. Why? Because they thought He was only a human being. They did not–and could not–believe He was God in the flesh, for in their minds, God would never lower Himself and assume a human body. This was inconceivable to them. Moreover, the Pharisees were so busy trying to get everyone to comply with the 613 commandments (mitzvot) and being faithful to the Torah and the many Kosher regulations they had so that Messiah would come and free them from the Romans that they were not following the "Spirit of the Law": the principles behind the Ten Commandments and the more important precepts of the Law (see 2 Cor 3:6; Mt 23:23-28); nor were they in tune with them, especially the prophecies regarding the promised Heavenly Messiah. If they had been fully aware of their true meaning, they would have known that Jesus was indeed the promised Messiah.

A reference to the Heavenly Messiah, a very unique one, is found in Psalm 110:1, where we find David saying: "The Lord says to my lord: 'Sit at my right hand, till I make your enemies your footstool.' " The first Lord mentioned here must be a reference to either God the Father or God the Holy Spirit (since it is the Spirit Who spoke through the Prophets), and the second Lord mentioned is a reference to Jesus, the Lord of lords, a descendant of David and the Messiah. Jesus mentioned this specific passage from the OT to the Pharisees in order to question them about the Messiah:

"When some Pharisees gathered together, Jesus asked them, 'What do you think about the Messiah? Whose descendant is he?' 'He is David's descendant,' they answered. 'Why, then,' Jesus asked, 'did the Spirit inspire David to call him "Lord"? David said, "The Lord said to my Lord: sit here at my right side until I put your enemies under your feet." 'If, then, David called him "Lord," how can the Messiah be David's descendant?' No one was able to give Jesus any answer, and from that day on, no one dared to ask him any more questions" (Mt 22:41-46; NCSB).

Note that instead of asking the Sadducees or scribes this extremely important question, Jesus asked the Pharisees who *they* thought the Messiah was, and most likely because He knew the Pharisees did not know the correct interpretation of the Messianic prophecies and had been spreading the false "Earthly messiah" teaching to the people for a long time. And yet, Jesus chose a Pharisee, Saul (St. Paul), one of the worst of all the Pharisees, to spread the Gospel to the Gentiles! How fitting!

Although a little difficult to see because the OT Messianic prophecies are not explicit and somewhat obscure, all of them proclaim, in one way or another, that the Messiah God promised to the Jews was going to be a Heavenly Messiah and not an Earthly messiah as the Pharisees and Essenes misinterpreted Him to be. Jesus, the promised Messiah, was and is "the Lion of the tribe of Judah, the Root of David." [11] He was going to be the actual Son of God, both divine and human, in one Person: the Son of God who became a man through the power of the Holy Spirit, possessing a Divine Nature, [12] and the Son of man through Mary, possessing a human nature. [13] Two natures in One Divine Person! (See chapter 4 for a fuller explanation.)

The chief priests—and especially the Pharisees—succeeded in getting the crowd present at Christ's arrest to side with them and condemn Jesus when Pilate presented Him to them: "Now the chief priests and the elders persuaded the people to ask for Barab'bas and destroy Jesus" (Mt 27:20). After Pilate had Jesus scourged, he asked the crowd what they wanted him to do with Jesus, and the crowd answered, "We have a law, and by that law he ought to die, because he has made himself the Son of God" (Jn 19:7). Who in the crowd do you suppose was yelling this? Sounds like the Pharisees and Sadducees to me! From another angle, the crowd asked for the release of the rebel Barab'bas—instead of Jesus—because Barab'bas represented the "Earthly messiah" to them, the type of messiah they were waiting for, the one who might free them from Roman rule. Nevertheless, the core of the Messianic Secret had obviously worked and Jesus was on His way to complete the Mission His Father had given to Him: a Mission of Love that would take Him to Calvary for OUR sake.

Only the Pharisees, Sadducees, scribes and the Elders had problems with Jesus. BIG problems. The Romans did not have a problem with Jesus; Jesus was not an enemy of the Romans. Pilate even said as much: "After he [Pilate] had said this, he went out to the Jews again, and told them, '**I find no crime in him**' " (Jn 18:38) [my emph.]. Scripture tells us Jesus never apologized to the Pharisees, Sadducees and scribes when He offended them, and rightly so for they deserved it. In today's politically correct American society, Jesus would be "thrown under the bus" many times over and surely silenced by the social media giants for everything He said to them. One example: "Then the disciples came and said to him, 'Do you know that the Pharisees were offended when they heard this saying?' He answered, 'Every plant which my heavenly Father has not planted will be rooted up. Let them alone; they are blind guides. And if a blind man leads a blind man, both will fall into a pit' " (Mt 15:12-14).

The Need For A New Religion

What happened to the promised Heavenly Messiah when He finally came? Since the Jews failed to realize that Jesus was the Heavenly Messiah sent by God the Father, particularly the Pharisees, Essenes, Sadducees, scribes and Elders, many of these urged and instigated Pontius Pilate to crucify Him because He claimed to be God. Undoubtedly, the chief priests (Sadducees), the Pharisees, the Essenes, the Elders, and the scribes were NOT going to go out into the world - after Christ's Death and Resurrection - and preach the Good News: the Gospel of Salvation only through Jesus Christ. It is very obvious as recorded in Scripture that they would not have done that - and in fact did not do that. Moreover, many of these still hated the followers of Christ ("Christians" as they were called then) after His Resurrection and even made up lies about Jesus not rising from the dead (Mt 28:11-15). They even persecuted and stoned to death some of the first Christians (Acts 6:8-15; 7:1-60). Saul, a Pharisee, who later

42

became known as St. Paul, was one of those in charge of the persecutions and stonings (Acts 8:1-3).

And if that is not enough, after the Apostles were put in prison by Cai'aphas and the Pharisees because they were attracting a large crowd – like Jesus had done – with their healings and expelling of demons, an angel came, released them from prison, and told them to go preach at the Temple, and when they were discovered and returned to Cai'aphas, he told them: "We strictly charged you not to teach in this [Jesus'] name, yet here you have filled Jerusalem with your teaching and **you intend to bring this man's blood upon us**.... they beat them and charged them not to speak in the name of Jesus" (Acts 5:28, 40) [my emph.]. After instigating Pilate repeatedly to crucify Jesus, even telling him: "His blood be on us and on our children!" (Mt 27:25), Cai'aphas now claims they are innocent of Jesus' blood? I can't imagine a more irresponsible, cowardly, patently false and egregious thing to say! Jesus was so right when He called them all those names: "Woe to you, scribes and Pharisees, hypocrites! for you are like whitewashed tombs, which outwardly appear beautiful, but within they are full of dead men's bones and all uncleanness. So you also outwardly appear righteous to men, but within you are full of hypocrisy and iniquity" (Mt 23:27-28).

A clarification here is in order regarding Judaism. The reader should not assume that I am promoting antisemitism when I stated that Judaism became obsolete with the coming of Christ and was supplanted by Catholicism as the religion through which salvation is to be obtained. Antisemitism is prejudice against or hatred of the Jewish people, which is quite different. "Semites" refers to certain peoples, notably Jews (Arabs are also Semites). Judaism however, is a religion, not a people. Please take note.

God came to Earth in the Person of Jesus Christ to establish a brand NEW Covenant with all mankind and seal it with HIS Blood, not with the blood of an innocent animal (see Heb 9:11-15), and consequently, also a brand NEW religion, a new Church, whose members, Catholics, the "New Chosen people" so to speak, would spread out into all parts of the world and preach the Good News of Salvation through Him for the Eternal Benefit of mankind. If the Jews had accepted Christ as the Messiah and Redeemer of mankind, Judaism would have been the "Catholic" religion for all to follow, but evidently, that is not what happened. God does not want us to practice a religion that is still waiting for the Messiah when He already came! Thus, Catholicism became the New and True Religion to follow on Earth from Christ forward. The Old Judaic Covenant was supplanted by Christ's New Covenant (see Heb 8:6-13).

Further evidence that Christ established a new religion, when Christ told His Apostles "I **will** build **my Church**" (Mt 16:18), this obviously meant a NEW Church, a NEW religion, because Judaism with its Second Temple and synagogues already existed and had been established for quite some time. So, the "Church" Jesus was building was a Brand New One, [14] a Universal one. Since the Jews rejected Jesus, He saw the need to prescribe new doctrines and new modes of worship and that meant a new religion. (Catholicism is the "portal" through which one can enter Heaven after death.) This is why Judaism was no longer to be followed by anyone with the coming of Christ, and this included the Jews. After Christ's Ascension, the Apostles went to the Temple and told the Jews to convert to the new religion (Acts 3:1-26; 4:1-4), and Jesus had forewarned them that they would be beaten in the synagogues for trying to convert the Jews to the new religion (Mk 13:9; Acts 5:40-42). Some say, "Just because we reject Jesus doesn't mean we also reject the Father in Heaven," but they are wrong, for Jesus said: "He who hears you hears me, and he who rejects you rejects me, and **he who rejects me rejects him who sent me**" [the Father] (Lk 10:16) [my emph.]. And in John we find: "....the Father loves the Son, and has given all things into his hand. He who believes in the Son has eternal life; he who does not **obey** the Son shall not see life, but the wrath of God rests upon him. [...] He who does not honor the Son does not honor the Father who sent him" (Jn 3:35-36; 5:23) [my emph.]. Jesus Himself said: "...no one comes to the Father, but by me" (Jn 14:6). Many Jewish authorities believed in Jesus: "Nevertheless many even of the authorities believed in him, but for fear of the Pharisees they did not confess it, lest they should be put out of the synagogue: for they loved the praise of men more than the praise of God" (Jn 12:42-43).

Many intelligent, smart and reasonable people are not aware that Catholicism is the only true religion on Earth because they haven't taken the time to study the world's religions and their origins, but once they do, it will become very clear. Now some will say: "What if you are wrong about Catholicism being the only true religion?" And my answer would be, "I cannot be wrong, because Christ taught this to be true, and since He is God, I know God does not lie and knows what He is talking about." The point is not that I might be wrong, but that it is impossible for God to be wrong. That is why I follow only Him and the Catholic religion He established.

Chapter 6

CONCLUSION

On page 957 of "A New Catholic Commentary On Holy Scripture" by Thomas Nelson Publishers, 1984, it is noted that two German Lutheran theologians, Georg William Wrede (1859-1906) and Rudolf Bultmann (1884-1976) believed the Apostle Mark invented the messianic secret (that Jesus never said any of this) and added it to his Gospel to serve as the only reason why Jesus had not been recognized as the Messiah, the Son of God, by the Jews. Wrede published this view in 1901.[15] This same Commentary also notes that the English Methodist theologian, Vincent Taylor (1887–1968) disagreed with this view and believed that Jesus' true identity was not revealed to the public until after the completion of His Mission (Death and Resurrection) because this was His "Destiny" see Mk 9:9); i.e., in order to ensure the completion of His Mission, which accords with St. Bede, St. Paul (1 Cor 2:6-9), and St. Remigius as noted earlier (see pp. 17-18). In my humble opinion, it is highly doubtful if not quite impossible that the Apostle Mark intentionally inserted such lies - regardless of good intentions - about his Lord in his Gospel considering the consequences thereof, and moreover, that both Matthew and Luke copied Mark in this untruth (Mark's Gospel was written first). Nevertheless, it does not surprise me that the two Protestant theologians in mention allowed their imaginations to run wild in this regard; it certainly was neither the first nor the last time wild Scriptural speculation has appeared from that side of the tracks. (Bultmann claimed the Gospels were "mythology.")

Since Jesus knew of the plot to kill Him (Jn 7:1), timing was of the utmost importance to Him, to the Master of

Time, so He avoided getting caught by the Pharisees and be executed before the Appointed Time. Jesus wanted things to go His way; be arrested when He was ready to be arrested; be condemned when He was ready to be condemned; and be executed when He was ready to be executed, and not before; namely, on the Passover Festival of April 3rd, 33 A.D.,[16] which would coincide with the Sabbath that particular year (see Jn 19:31). Like everything else He does so well, Jesus willingly and skillfully directed His own destiny and only admitted His divinity and Messiahship after Peter's declaration (Mt 16.16) because His execution was imminent. The Lord, Master, and Creator of the Universe directed all events around Him as a Conductor directs a Symphony, with the exception that the players did not know what notes they were going to play next.

The combination of the Three Contributing Factors with the Messianic Secret reveals why the Jewish people did not believe and thereby accept Jesus Christ as the foretold Heavenly Messiah that He was then and still is now, a chronic lack of faith that continues to this day in all forms of Rabbinic Judaism with the exception of the movement "Messianic Jews" (or other similar groups): a religious belief system that fatally contradicts itself and therefore cannot be taken seriously. Mixing Rabbinic Judaism and Catholicism does not work; it is futile to do that. You either practice Judaism or Catholicism but not both at the same time. The reason is Rabbinic Judaism and Catholicism are two separate and distinct religions that have conflicting beliefs, so you can't mix these religions together if their beliefs conflict with one another. For example, at the top of the list is the fact that in Catholicism, Jesus is both man and God in one divine Person. Rabbinic Judaism teaches that is not true. That's conflict number one. Number two, Rabbinic Judaism teaches that there's no such thing as

Original Sin, and Catholicism teaches that there is. Number three, Catholicism teaches that Jesus died to redeem the entire human race, while Rabbinic Judaism teaches that is not true. Number four, Catholicism teaches that Mary, the mother of Jesus, was born without the "stain" of Original Sin, and since Jews don't believe in Original Sin, they don't believe that Catholic tenet either, and so on. So you see, it is very easy to prove that you can't mix both of them together and come up with a logical and coherent religion to practice because they conflict with one another. Incidentally, many practices in Judaism became obsolete with the coming of Christ.

Speaking In Parables and The Road To Emma'us

"And he said, 'Go, and say to this people: 'Hear and hear, but do not understand; see and see, but do not perceive'" (Is 6:9).

There is an interesting link between Jesus speaking in parables to the crowds and the Road to Emma'us incident, and it has to do with Jesus being the Heavenly Messiah and not the Earthly messiah the Jews had been waiting for. In regards to the parables, in the Gospel of Matthew we find:

"Then the disciples came and said to him, 'Why do you speak to them in parables?' And he answered them, 'To you it has been given to know the secrets of the kingdom of heaven, but to them it has not been given' " (Mt 13:10-11). The main teaching here is that the "secrets" Jesus is talking about is He Himself. That God the Father would send to Earth His Son to redeem the human race was a "secret" of Heaven, a secret contained in a veiled way in the prophecies of the OT Prophets, but now, the "secret" is standing right in front of them! In person! "That is; With the hearing ye shall hear words, but shall not understand

48

the hidden meaning of those words; seeing ye shall see My flesh indeed, but shall not discern the divinity." [17]

Continuing with the Gospel of Matthew:

"For to him who has will more be given, and he will have abundance; but from him who has not, even what he has will be taken away. This is why I speak to them in parables, because seeing they do not see, and hearing they do not hear, nor do they understand. With them indeed is fulfilled the prophecy of Isaiah which says: 'You shall indeed hear but never understand, and you shall indeed see but never perceive' " [Is 6:9] (Mt 13:12-14).

In this passage, Jesus is saying that "him who has," that is, he who has faith and believes Jesus is the Son of God, the Heavenly Messiah (and not the Earthly messiah), more faith will be given to him, but he who does not have that Faith, even the little faith he does have will have it taken away because he is not worthy of it. The Jews are seeing and hearing the Heavenly Messiah, but they are not aware of that fact because they were not expecting him to be the Son of God in human form due in large part to the false messianic teachings of the Pharisees and the Essenes. "Whoso has the desire and the zeal, to him shall be given all those things which are of God; but whoso lacketh these, and does not contribute that part that pertains to him, to him neither are the things which are of God given, but even those things that he hath are taken from him; not because God takes them away, but because he hath made himself unworthy of those that he has." [18]

"Or, To the Apostles who believe in Christ, there is given, but from the Jews who believed not on the Son of God, there is taken away, even whatever good they might seem to have by nature. For they cannot understand anything

49

with wisdom, seeing they have not the head of wisdom." [19] "For by reason of the darkness of His discourse, they being blinded did not understand the Lord's sayings, and not understanding them, they did not believe on Him, and not believing on Him they crucified Him" [20] (see Jn 12:37).

"These things then which the Apostles saw and heard, are such as His presence, His voice, His teaching. And in this He sets them before not the evil only, but even before the good, pronouncing them more blessed than even the righteous men of old. For they saw not only what the Jews saw not, but also what the righteous men and Prophets desired to see, and had not seen. For they [the righteous and Prophets] had beheld these things only by faith, but these [Apostles and others] by sight, and even yet more clearly. You see how He identifies the OT with the New, for had the Prophets been the servants of any strange or hostile Deity, they would not have desired to see Christ." [21]

" 'For this people's heart has grown dull, and their ears are heavy of hearing and their eyes they have closed, lest they should perceive with their eyes, and hear with their ears, and understand with their heart, and turn for me to heal them.' But blessed are your eyes, for they see, and your ears, for they hear. Truly, I say to you, many Prophets and righteous men longed to see what you see, and did not see it, and to hear what you hear, and did not hear it" (Mt 13:15-17).

Jesus is saying in this passage that the hearts of the Jews had become "dull": not on fire and "burning" for the Lord anymore, and their ears are "heavy of hearing": they don't listen to God and don't obey Him, and "their eyes they have closed": they failed to understand the Messianic prophecies because they were reduced to nationalistic aspirations by primarily the Pharisees, and all of these are now preventing them from "seeing" (the "log" in their eye) and recognizing the True and Heavenly Messiah that is right in front of them, speaking to them in person (see Acts 28:25-31). The righteous men and Prophets of old once longed for the privilege and opportunity to have seen and heard the Messiah in person as they all are seeing and hearing Him now. "Or, He is speaking of the blessedness of the Apostolic times, to whose eyes and ears it was permitted to see and to hear the salvation of God, many Prophets and just men having desired to see and to hear that which was destined to be in the fullness of times." [22]

The true identity of Christ was not known for certain, not even by His Apostles, until after His Resurrection from the dead, and even then, some of His disciples had doubts. The Gospel of Luke contains a passage, a very popular passage, that reveals this truth.

"That very day two of them were going to a village named Emma'us, about seven miles from Jerusalem, and talking with each other about all these things that had happened. While they were talking and discussing together, Jesus himself drew near and went with them. But their eyes were kept from recognizing him. And he said to them, 'What is this conversation which you are holding with each other as you walk?' And they stood still, looking sad. Then one of them, named Cle'opas, answered him, 'Are you the only visitor to Jerusalem who does not know the things that have happened there in these days?' And he said to them, 'What things?' And they said to him, 'Concerning Jesus of Nazareth, who was a **prophet** mighty in deed and word before God and all the people, and how our chief priests and rulers delivered him up to be condemned to death, and crucified him. **But we had hoped that he was the one to redeem Israel**. Yes, and besides all this, it is now the third day since this happened. Moreover, some women of our

51

company amazed us. They were at the tomb early in the morning and did not find his body; and they came back saying that they had even seen a vision of angels, who said that he was alive. Some of those who were with us went to the tomb, and found it just as the women had said; but him they did not see.' And he said to them, '**O foolish men, and slow of heart to believe all that the Prophets have spoken!** Was it not necessary that the Christ should suffer these things and enter into his glory?' **And beginning with Moses and all the Prophets, he interpreted to them in all the Scriptures the things concerning himself**.

"So they drew near to the village to which they were going. He appeared to be going further, but they constrained him, saying, 'Stay with us, for it is toward evening and the day is now far spent.' So he went in to stay with them. When he was at table with them, he took the bread and blessed and broke it, and gave it to them. And their eyes were opened and they recognized him; and he vanished out of their sight. They said to each other, '**Did not our hearts burn within us while he talked to us on the road, while he opened to us the Scriptures?**' And they rose that same hour and returned to Jerusalem; and they found the Eleven gathered together and those who were with them, who said, 'The Lord has risen indeed, and has appeared to Simon!' Then they told what had happened on the road, and how he was known to them in the breaking of the bread" (Lk 24:13-35) [my emph.].

The first odd thing to notice here is the word "prophet," that they considered Jesus a "prophet mighty in deed." This proves they were not aware that He was God in the flesh, the Son of God. And the second thing to notice here is, "we had hoped that he was the one to **redeem Israel**." The "redeeming of Israel" was synonymous with the liberation from Roman Rule led by the expected Earthly messiah.

This is proof that these two disciples – together with who knows how many others – were hoping that Jesus was going to be the expected Earthly messiah that would free Israel from Roman rule and domination. St. Thomas Aquinas notes: "For they expected that Christ would redeem Israel from the evils that were rising up among them **and the Roman slavery**" (Catena Aurea, St. Luke, p. 775, Theophyl; see Acts 1:6) [my emph.].

Jesus tells them how foolish they are for not understanding and "believing" the actual contents of the Messianic prophecies that spoke about a Heavenly Messiah and not an Earthly messiah. This is why Jesus "interpreted" and explained the Scriptural prophecies to them: to make them understand that the Earthly messiah the Jews were expecting, the one even they themselves had hoped Jesus was, was a gross misinterpretation of the Messianic prophecies: a reduction to nationalistic aspirations.

After Jesus gave them the correct interpretation of the prophecies, that He was not the Earthly messiah they had hoped He was ("...we had hoped that he was the one to redeem Israel"), their "hearts burned" within them by having the correct interpretation of the Scriptures and then knowing who Jesus **truly** was: the True Messiah and Son of the Living God who came to redeem the world, and not just the Jews. They also realized that Jesus, the one the Jews rejected and crucified, was indeed the foretold Heavenly Messiah and not the Earthly messiah the Pharisees had erroneously led the Jews to expect: a Pharisaic pseudo-messiah many Jews are sadly still waiting for to this day, and one that is never going to come, because Jesus Christ was AND IS the Prophesied Messiah who already came, completed His Mission, and went Home to our Father in Heaven to intercede for us daily.

It is interesting to note that these two persons on the road to Emma'us recognized it was Jesus "in the breaking of the bread" (Lk 24:31). How can this be? Cle'opas was not at the Last Supper when Jesus "Broke the Bread" for the first time, and the other individual with him was not an Apostle, for Scripture says that they both "returned to Jerusalem; and they found the Eleven gathered together and those who were with them" (Lk 24:33). Since it was only the Apostles who were with Jesus at the Last Supper when He Broke the Bread and instituted the Holy Eucharist for the first time, how did these two, who were not present at the Last Supper, put together the breaking of the bread with Jesus only three days later on the day of Resurrection? The answer may be that being disciples, they learned about the "Breaking of the Bread" from the Apostles sometime after the arrest of Jesus and before they started their Journey of Discovery on the Road to Emma'us. Moreover, while they were all together discussing all this in Jerusalem, Jesus appeared to them **again** and likewise "opened their minds to understand the Scriptures" (24:45). Clearly, Jesus was making sure they all understood that He was the prophesied Heavenly Messiah who came to redeem mankind and not just the Jews. But this "understanding" took some time, for in Acts 1:6, just before Jesus ascended into Heaven, the Apostles asked Him: "Lord, will you at this time restore the kingdom to Israel ?" (Free them from the Romans.) Therefore, they **still** did not understand what His Holy Mission on Earth was. Thank God He is so Loving and Patient. Very, very Loving and Patient.

It appears that Jesus' divinity remained a secret from the time of His birth and well into His public ministry when He was in His early 30s, and most likely never performed miracles as a child, as an adolescent, or even as an adult prior to His public ministry except perhaps in the private company of His parents, Mary and Joseph. This is somewhat confirmed by the fact that when Jesus read the Scriptures in the synagogue in Nazareth where He grew up, they all wondered, "Where did this man get this wisdom and these mighty works? Is not this the carpenter's son?" (Mt 13:54-55). In other words, "Isn't he just like one of us, an ordinary person?" Evidently, His parents kept His divinity a secret and for good reason, yet Mary knew He possessed supernatural powers as revealed at the Wedding at Cana (Jn 2:1-12). Further proof of this well-kept secret is also found in the "Walk to Emmaus" in the Gospel of Luke. Here, one of the two walking on the road is named Cle'opas, and Cle'opas refers to Jesus as a "prophet mighty in deed and word" (Lk 24:19). According to various sources, Cle'opas was the "brother" of Joseph, the legal father of Jesus who raised Him from birth. So, if Cle'opas, a close family member, did not know that Jesus was a divine Person, it is because Joseph and Mary did not reveal this to their family members, and much less, to anyone else. (Prophets were not divine Persons.) It was very important to keep Jesus' divinity a secret while He was growing up. In this light, it is now easy to see why Mary got upset with the boy Jesus after spending three days looking for Him and finally finding Him in the Temple (Lk 2:48), perhaps Mary and Joseph were very worried that His divinity would be discovered without them there to prevent the exposure of that secret; one they had kept for so long. In v. 51, it says that after they found Him, Jesus "was obedient to them," most likely after they reminded Him of the importance of keeping that secret. In fact, Jesus, as an adult, kept this secret for quite some time, gradually revealing it to His Apostles. Incredible as it sounds, many still don't know He is God! Still a secret?

Eucharistic Miracles

There is one particular supernatural phenomena that is unique to Catholicism which is not found in any Protestant denomination and for that matter in any other religion in the world. Moreover, it is at the center of Catholicism and Catholic worship: the Holy Eucharist. The Eucharist (also called the "host") is a round thin piece of unleavened bread, made from wheat flour and water that is consumed at the end of all Catholic Masses by the faithful. The Catholic Church teaches that Jesus changed bread and wine into his body and blood at the Last Supper with the words: "This is my body" and "This is my blood" (cf. Mt 26:26-28) for the spiritual nourishment of His Apostles, and this has been repeated ever since at all Catholic Masses since the Ascension of Christ into Heaven 2000 years ago for the spiritual nourishment of all Catholics. Many Protestants, however, do not believe the Catholic Eucharist is the actual body and blood of Christ but is only a "symbol" instead. Both Scripture and modern science provide plenty of evidence in defense of Christ's divinity, and in regards to the latter, results from incontrovertible analyses of Eucharistic miracles is opening the eyes of even hard core atheists.

One example (of many) is found in the book, "A Cardiologist Examines Jesus," by Dr. Franco Serafini. On pages 49-50 is a detailed account of a scientific analysis of a sample taken from a consecrated Catholic host (made from unleavened wheat flour) that had miraculously turned into living flesh in an Argentinian Roman Catholic church in 1996. One analysis of this miraculous host was performed on April 20, 2004 by "Prof. Frederick Zugibe, chief medical examiner and cardiologist in Rockland County in New York. His academic profile, made up of scientific discoveries and numerous publications, together with his thirty-year experience of ten thousand autopsies, is impressive at the very least."

Looking at the sample under a microscope, unaware of what it was (they did not tell him), Dr. Zugibe said: "I am a heart specialist. The heart is *my business.* This is heart muscle tissue, coming from the left ventricle, near a valvular area. This cardiac muscle is inflamed; it has lost its striations and is infiltrated by leukocytes." Since leukocytes can only exist in a living organism, the sample he was looking at was a "living" sample (it was already eight (8) years old!). When Dr. Zugibe was asked, "How long would these leukocytes survive for, if the tissue were set in water." This sample from the miraculous host had been kept in a vial filled with distilled water since 2001, for three years. "They would dissolve within a few minutes and no longer exist," was his reply. When he was finally told what the sample was and how it had been kept until then, Dr. Zugibe exclaimed: "Absolutely incredible! Inexplicable by science!" Unbeknownst to him, the piece of heart muscle he had examined belonged to God Himself, Jesus the Christ. "Blessed are those who have not seen and yet believe" (Jn 20:29). This is incontrovertible scientific proof that the Holy Eucharist IS the actual body, blood, soul and divinity of Jesus Christ. In his book, Dr. Franco Serafini adds that the examined flesh/host contained human blood, white blood cells, red blood cells undergoing autolysis, hemoglobin, leukocytes, and that the flesh itself had miraculously remained alive for years, even to this very day! And this is only one of many documented cases. For more read "Eucharistic Miracles," by Joan Carroll Cruz. These are miracles that God gives to mankind in order to draw souls to His one and only Holy Mother Church, the Catholic Church. Other miracles with the same purpose are listed in the book "The Incorruptibles," also by Joan Carroll Cruz. Here, Catholic saints who have passed away, some of them hundreds of years ago, were found to be without corruption and appear to be only sleeping after exhumation.

Since the Eucharist is the very body, blood, soul, and divinity of God in the Person of Jesus Christ, it is therefore the most valuable item on Earth! And best of all, we can obtain it free of charge with only one condition: we must be a member of the Catholic Church in "good standing," that is, in the "state of grace": free of grave (mortal) sin. Nothing else on Earth can compare in value to the Holy Eucharist; not money, jewels, real estate, or power of any kind. The special value of the Eucharist was given to mankind personally by Jesus Christ Himself.

The Holy Roman Catholic Church is the only Christian "Church," per se, whose history can be traced back to Jesus Christ and His Apostles. The only one. It is the original Christian Church established c. 33 A.D. by God Himself in the Person of Jesus Christ: both God and man in one Divine Person. The first recorded use of the word "Catholic," which means "universal," is attributed to St. Ignatius of Antioch c. 110 A.D. So, from around 110 A.D. forward, the name Catholic has been used to refer to the Church Jesus Christ founded for the benefit of mankind, and specifically "Roman Catholic" to refer to the original Catholic Church Jesus established with Peter as its first Pope followed by successive popes to the present Pope Francis, the 267th Pope and leader of the Roman Catholic Church.

The very fact that Christ came back from the dead and the Pharisees, Sadducees and scribes continued their unbelief and even persecuted the followers of Christ is quite remarkable but not surprising. Jesus gave His disciples and followers a parable in this regard that reveals how stubborn people can be in believing, even when faced with an absolute truth:

"There was a rich man, who was clothed in purple and fine linen and who feasted sumptuously every day. And at his gate lay a poor man named Laz'arus, full of sores, who desired to be fed with what fell from the rich man's table; moreover the dogs came and licked his sores. The poor man died and was carried by the angels to Abraham's bosom. The rich man also died and was buried; and in Hades, being in torment, he lifted up his eyes, and saw Abraham far off and Laz'arus in his bosom. And he called out, 'Father Abraham, have mercy upon me, and send Laz'arus to dip the end of his finger in water and cool my tongue; for I am in anguish in this flame.' But Abraham said, 'Son, remember that you in your lifetime received your good things, and Laz'arus in like manner evil things; but now he is comforted here, and you are in anguish. And besides all this, between us and you a great chasm has been fixed, in order that those who would pass from here to you may not be able, and none may cross from there to us.' And he said, 'Then I beg you, father, to send him to my father's house, for I have five brothers, so that he may warn them, lest they also come into this place of torment.' But Abraham said, 'They have Moses and the prophets; let them hear them.' And he said, 'No, father Abraham; but if someone goes to them from the dead, they will repent.' He said to him, 'If they do not hear Moses and the prophets, **neither will they be convinced if someone should rise from the dead**' " [namely Jesus] (Lk 16:19-31) [my emph.].

I personally believe Jesus referred to Himself as "Son of man" for two main reasons: (1) to conceal His divinity (vs. Son of God); (2) to prevent the titles "messiah" and "king" from being assigned to him by the Jews who were expecting an Earthly messiah/king to free them from Roman rule (cf. Jn 6:15). The Catholic Encyclopedia (under "Son of man") states that in the time of Christ, the

59

term Son of man was not widely known as a Messianic title, and since Jesus wanted to keep His divine identity a secret, this may be one reason why He frequently used this term when referring to Himself: to keep the focus on His humanity. In the Gospel of Mark alone, "Son of man" appears 14 times. The Messianic Secret, together with the Three Contributing Factors, ensured the success of God's Holy Will: Jesus Christ's Sacrifice on the Cross to redeem mankind. The Redemption of the human race required the sacrificial death of God incarnate. Why such a high price? Nothing else was capable of restoring the broken relationship between God and man due to Adam and Eve's Original Sin of disobedience. That's how serious the sin of disobedience to God was – and is! Father Leslie Rumble noted: "God willed that the scales of justice should be balanced, and for that a man had to die for the sin of man" (Radio Replies, # 439, p. 228). Thus, God's Son, through Mary, became man, and through His death atoned for the sin of man. (For more on this see "Why Jesus Had To Die For Our Sins," p. 146.)

But why did Jesus have to die to atone for mankind? Was there no other way? St. Paul said: "Indeed, under the law almost everything is purified with blood, and **without the shedding of blood there is no forgiveness of sins**" (Heb 9:22) [my emph.]. The fact Jesus willingly died for us proves the immensity of God's Supreme Love for us: "Greater love has no man than this, that a man lay down his life for his friends" (Jn 15:13). Since God the Father created all things through, with, and in His Son, it was therefore fitting and proper that the work of the Redemption of mankind would be performed by Him. Among other things, the Book of Revelation clearly shows how Christ calls mankind to repentance and conversion in order to save us from Eternal Hell after death, for He came to Earth and died on the Cross 2000 years ago to restore the

60

broken relationship between man and God and open the closed Gates of Heaven for everyone because of the Supreme Love He has for every single one of us. And the easiest and surest way to get to Heaven is to remain united to Him: to obey Him and follow His teachings through the Catholic Church He established. There is no other or better way to get to Heaven. God the Father ordains the world through the New Covenant established by His Son, Jesus Christ, who "paid the price" with His own blood and "bought" us back from the devil's possession, but the devil, the world, and the weakness of our own flesh can be—and are—obstacles on our way to Heaven that we have to overcome until we finally leave this world through death's door and enter Heaven for all Eternity. If we don't listen to God, if we don't obey Him and follow the Catholic Church He established, chances are we won't make it. So, why take a chance? Do the right thing and obey God today! While there is still Time. Time can be an enemy or a friend. Choose the latter.

"Therefore gird up your minds, be sober, set your hope fully upon the grace that is coming to you at the revelation of Jesus Christ. As obedient children, do not be conformed to the passions of your former ignorance, but as he who called you is holy, be holy yourselves in all your conduct; since it is written, You shall be holy, for I am holy. [...] And by this we may be sure that we know him, if we keep his commandments. He who says I know him but disobeys his commandments is a liar, and the truth is not in him; but whoever keeps his word, in him truly love for God is perfected. By this we may be sure that we are in him: he who says he abides in him ought to walk in the same way in which he walked. [...] A man who governs his passions is master of his world. We must either command them or be enslaved by them. It is better to be a hammer than an anvil" (1 Peter 1:13-16; 1 John 2:3-6; St. Dominic). When I stated

61

earlier that Jesus established a New Religion for all to follow in order to merit Salvation and go to Heaven, this is all true. However, keep in mind that Catholicism and Judaism are intimately linked since Catholicism is the "perfection" of Judaism. This is why Catholicism embodies many Judaic elements within it. The Jews erroneously believed the Messiah was coming to save only them when He was actually coming to redeem the entire human race. Those who accept this truth and join the Church He established are known as Catholics. But this doesn't mean those who practiced and are practicing Judaism will not be saved, for St. Paul said: "…a hardening has come upon part of Israel, until the full number of the Gentiles come in, and so all Israel will be saved [...] For the gifts and the call of God are irrevocable" (Rom 11:25, 26, 29).

It is good to want to go to Heaven and enjoy eternal life in perfect bliss and happiness forever, but many do not know or want to believe that they need to be saved to get there. A lot of people are not aware of Original Sin and their sinfulness. Many think they'll get to Heaven without religion, without help from anyone. Some say: "I am a better person than those religious nuts." This is false pride: "God opposes the proud, but gives grace to the humble" (Jas 4:6). Men don't like humbling themselves, and less, being humbled by anyone. They'd rather enjoy the pleasures this world can give them here and now instead of giving them up for the pleasures God offers in a future life. They are blind to the dire and horrifying consequences of their sins. Jesus said: "He who loves his life [on Earth] loses it [in Hell], and he who hates his life in this world will keep it for eternal life [in Heaven]" (Jn 12:25; my emph.). Very Sobering Facts!

"To use this life well is the pathway through death to everlasting life." (St. John Almond)

Endnotes

1. Cf. *Catena Aurea* (*CA*), Luke, p. 169. Bede; *CA,* Luke, p. 170. Bede; cf. 1 Cor 2:6-9.

2. https://www.newadvent.org/cathen/14144a.htm.

3. www.jewishvirtuallibrary.org/judaism-s-rejection-of-original-sin; www.jewishvirtuallibrary.org/jews-for-jesus.

4. www.jewishvirtuallibrary.org/pharisees-sadducees-and-essenes.

5. www.jewishvirtuallibrary.org/the-messiah.

6. *CA*, Vol II, St Mark, p. 30. Theophyl.

7. www.catholic.org/saints/saint.php?saint_id=376.

8. *Radio Replies* (*RR*), Fr. Leslie Rumble, # 374-75, p. 203; # 376, p. 204; # 379, p. 205; # 380, p. 206.

9. *RR*, # 142, p. 96.

10. *CA*, Vol II, St Mark, p. 29. Theophyl.

11. Rv. 5:5.

12. Lk. 1:34-35.

13. Lk. 1:26-35.

14. See *RR*, # 123, p. 86; # 124, p. 87; # 125, p. 87.

15. *The Messianic Secret*, William Wrede. Cambridge: James Clarke & Co., 1971.
16. www.ncregister.com/search?q=when+Jesus+died.

17. *CA*, Volume 1, St. Mt., Part 1, p. 486. Gloss.

18. *CA*, Volume 1, St. Mt., Part 1, p. 485. Chrys.

19. *CA*, Volume 1, St. Mt., Part 1, p. 485. Jerome.

20. *CA*, Volume 1, St. Mt., Part 1, p. 488-89 Aug.

21. *CA*, Volume 1, St. Mt., Part 1, p. 490. Chrys.

22. *CA*, Volume 1, St. Mt., Part 1, p. 489. Hilary.

About the Author

Juan Novo was born in Habana Cuba seven years before the communist Castro regime took totalitarian control of this burgeoning island paradise and turned it into an isolated, run down specter of her former glory. He came to the U.S.A. unaccompanied when he was nine years old through "Operation Pedro Pan," a clandestine operation that succeeded in rescuing over 14,000 unaccompanied Cuban minor children from communist indoctrination and control by the communist Castro regime. The operation, which ended with the Cuban Missile Crisis in 1962, was run and directed by Monsignor Bryan O. Walsh of the Catholic Welfare Bureau in Miami, Florida.

By the time he was nineteen, Juan had become a professional musician and was making a living as a percussionist playing music in the San Francisco area under contract to Warner Brothers Studios in a band called "Fat City." In 1976, he graduated from Spokane Falls Community College with degrees in both music theory and musical instrument repair and restorations and has been active as a practicing professional technician in this field for the past 50 years.

Mr. Novo founded the Research and Development Committee for the National Association of Professional Band Instrument Repair Technicians (NAPBIRT) in 1983, and it was here where he was "bit" for the first time by the "investigative writing bug." Juan ended up publishing a work entitled "The Grenadilla Story," an in-depth investigative study of African Blackwood, an African hardwood that has been used to make woodwind musical instruments for over a century. The report revealed the precious wood was at the edge of extinction which led to successful replanting programs years later. Mr. Novo has written technical repair and restoration articles published in the Association's trade journal, "TechniCom." His work with musical instruments has been featured in several TV specials, and articles about him and his work have appeared in both foreign and domestic newspapers, magazines, and periodicals. Although Juan switched careers and entered the musical instrument repair field full time in 1976, he continued to play percussion as a hobby and has performed in concerts with Jazz legends such as the late Dizzy Gillespie and Ira Sullivan.

Since 1983, Mr. Novo has been making professional model Grenadilla wood mouthpieces for the metal concert flute which are played by both amateur and professional flutists worldwide. Between 1981 and 1984, Mr. Novo was awarded two U.S. patents on musical instrument designs. One of these, patent # 4,685,373, is for the transparent FANTASIA flute he invented in 1984: a professional grade transparent flute that is illuminated with colored lights during performance. The first such instrument, built in 1985, was commissioned by the late Julius Baker, principal flautist for the New York Philharmonic Orchestra. This instrument was later purchased by the late New York Latin-Jazz flutist Dave Valentin and is featured in one of his albums entitled, "Light Struck." The FANTASIA flute made U.S. Patent history, for it was the first illuminated musical wind instrument to be awarded a patent by the U.S. Patent Office. As a result, a new division had to be created for it and it remains to this day the only such instrument in its class.

In the late 80s, Juan served for a time as editor of the "Sunshine Jazz Messenger," the newsletter for Miami's Sunshine Jazz Organization, and in 1990, his Grenadilla flute mouthpiece, played by Dave Valentin, was featured in the soundtrack of the film "Havana" starring Robert

66

Redford. His books, "A Race Redeemed," and "Who Do *You* Say I Am?" are Mr. Novo's latest and most important investigative works. Juan is a practicing Catholic, a member of the Knights of Columbus, and an avid student of Catholic theology and philosophy.

Made in the USA
Columbia, SC
24 November 2024

46987092R00039